Hengistbury Head

Geology and History

by

Bill Rees

Chalk Ridge Publications

©*Bill Rees 2001*

ISBN 0-9542907-0-4

2nd Print Master, correcting typographical errors 29/08/2002

Published and Printed in England by

Chalk Ridge Publications,
17 Howard Road,
Bournemouth,
Dorset,
BH8 9DZ

British Library Cataloguing-In-Publication Data
A catalogue record for this book is available from the British Library.

Contents

Pictures *(centre pages)*

Bibliography

Hengistbury Head
Edited by C.S. Pepin MA 1967

A Natural History of Bournemouth and District
Edited Daniel Morris D.Sc 1915

Hengistbury Head, The Coast
Peter Hawes 1998

Christchurch Harbour
Mike Powell 1995

The Hengistbury Head Nature trail
Peter Hawes and Mark Holloway
1990

Smuggling in Poole, Bournemouth and Neighbourhood
B.C. Short 1927

18th Century Smuggling in Christchurch
Allen White 1973

Hengistbury Head
Barry Cunliffe 1976

Hengistbury Head Archaeology Trail
Peter Hawes and Mark Holloway 1994

Mudeford Sandbank News &
Hengistbury Head Times magazines
Editor Tim Baber

Introduction

I came to write this small book after each of my four children had to do a project on Hengistbury Head as part of their school studies. Their research touched on the fascinating history of this beautiful place, and showed me how little I knew about the history or structure of this area. I have lived here for most of my life and I must admit that the local history and geology of Bournemouth and the surrounding area was a closed book to me.

Initially I published this as a web site. The original site may be found at web address:
www.hengistbury.head.btinternet.co.uk

This address may however change as time goes on, but a search engine such as Yahoo! should be able to find it (search on "Hengistbury Head").

After I published the web site a number of people contacted me asking if I could produce the information from the web site in hard copy, well, here it is! The format is necessarily somewhat different but I hope the essence of the web site is maintained.

Most of this information has been gleaned from other publications and personal observation. The publications range from academic, historical, and amateur, some dating back many years, others only recently published. I have included a list of these books in the bibliography. Another great resource has been the Red House Museum in Christchurch where the staff are ever helpful and have provided a veritable mountain of data about Hengistbury Head.

Many people visit the Head, climb to the summit, admire the view and leave without appreciating the other less well trodden areas. Only a few understand why it is crumbling into the sea. I only really began to appreciate the many different aspects to the Hengistbury Head after beginning this small project and was quite dismayed to find that the catastrophic erosion is mainly the result of man.

I hope this book will provide an outline of the many different facets to Hengistbury Head's geology and history and provide a reasonable starting point for anyone else who wishes to study one or more of the many aspects of this place. I am strictly of "amateur status" and while I hope this book is both useful and accurate I do apologise for any unforeseen foul-ups!

Next time you are at Hengistbury Head why not vary your route, try the northern shore, crossing the bridge over Holloway's cut to Mudeford spit, or follow the route of the Noddy train through the quiet lowland marshes and stunted forest on the northern shore. Of course there are always the magnificent views from the top of Warren Hill or the beautiful southern beach along with its sad crumbling cliffs. Look out for the Ironstones either on the beach, beginning to naturally reform Hengistbury Head's sea defences or still embedded in the cliff face. Always treat her with care. The weak sandstone and thin soil is easily damaged and may never repair. She is too nice to lose.

Kind Regards

Bill Rees 2001
e-mail:hengistbury.head@btinternet.com or bill_rees@yahoo.co.uk

Hengistbury Head, An Outline

Hengistbury Head is a 35 metre high sandstone headland approximately one and a half kilometres in length. It stands half way between the entrance to Poole Harbour and Hirst spit on the south coast of England. It forms the main division between Poole and Christchurch Bays. The initial formation of Hengistbury Head dates back approximately 60 million years although newer alluvial based deposits have been laid down as well and the later of these date back less than 10,000 years. In fact new deposits are still being laid down. Until comparatively recent geological time, Hengistbury Head was several kilometres inland.

Hengistbury Head forms a natural breakwater protecting a small natural harbour formed in its lee from the prevailing south-westerly wind. A long sand spit has formed trailing off the end of Hengistbury Head . This sandspit forms the easterly perimeter of Christchurch Harbour. The sand spit is known under several names including Mudeford spit, Mudeford beach and locally (as I remember from my youth as the Island. Without Hengistbury Head it is probable that most of the town of Christchurch and all of Christchurch Harbour would cease to exist. Poole Bay and Christchurch Bay would merge and become one.

Hengistbury Head had been subject to erosion ever since the southerly chalk ridge, that stretched from the Needles in the Isle of Wight to the Old Harry rocks near Studland, was breached by the sea. The sea invaded the river valley between the ridge and the Head and rapidly eroded the soft rocks to the south of the Head. This erosion was slowed, if not stopped, by the accumulation of hard Ironstone boulders that were left from the erosion of the softer rocks in which they were embedded. The rate of erosion has increased rapidly since the mid 19th century, when the Hengistbury Mining Company removed a great deal of the hard Ironstone boulders (known as Doggers) from the beach. They also dredged many thousands of tons of the Doggers from the inshore waters around the Head. These Doggers had formed a natural defence against the sea and their removal caused a very serious instability in the natural system that had developed and had kept the whole region relatively stable for at least 2000 years. Since the 1930's a great deal of time and effort has been put into rectifying the situation. Bournemouth Borough Council (formerly Bournemouth Corporation) has spent a great deal of money in the construction of breakwaters and groynes. While these schemes have generally been successful, almost half of Hengistbury Head, including one of the original promontories, has been lost.

Hengistbury Head was arguably the premier port for the import of continental goods, such as Italian wine, in around 100BC. Some have referred to it as the first truly urban settlement in England. The influence of the settlement at Hengistbury Head declined during Roman times and finally ended as the Romans left. Hengistbury Head has not been subject to human habitation for a considerable time although abandoned plans for house building and leisure development did have a significant effect upon the Head during the early part of the 20th century.

The archaeological and ecological importance of Hengistbury Head was formally recognised after a detailed archaeological survey (1915) conducted by Mr. Bushe-Fox. This survey was conducted as a direct result of the campaigning of a local historian named Herbert Druitt. Druitt had tirelessly sought to protect the Head after the ravages of the Hengistbury Mining Company. Hengistbury Head was purchased by Bournemouth Corporation in 1930 from Gordon

Selfridge. Selfridge had planned to build a mansion on the summit. At this time Hengistbury Head was suffering from catastrophic erosion and Selfridge had abandoned the planned development. Since then Hengistbury Head has been safe from building and industrial exploitation, although tourism has had a significant and detrimental effect upon the environment, especially where tourists have decided to leave the designated paths and scramble over the thin sandy escarpments. Many places on Hengistbury Head have crumbled and have been left denuded of vegetation.

Hengistbury Head has been designated a Site of Special Scientific Interest (SSSI) along with most of Christchurch Harbour and the lowland marshes of Stanpit that lie at the junction of the rivers Stour and Avon as they enter Christchurch Harbour.

Hengistbury Head is a beautiful timeless place. In the grand scheme of things Hengistbury Head is doomed to be washed into the sea. We are fortunate to be able to enjoy its windswept vista and admire the truly magnificent views across both Christchurch Harbour and out across the Solent. Try to treat her with care, then at least as many as is possible of the future generations may enjoy this natural spectacle as we do today.

The Geology of Hengistbury Head

The approach to Hengistbury Head starts approximately 7 metres above sea level, this being just west of the Iron Age defences known as the Double Dykes . About 150 metres east of the Double Dykes the headland rises steeply and starts to level off at about 30 metres. The Head is approximately 33 to 35 metres high at its highest point which is approximately 1/3rd of the way along or about 700 metres from its most easterly point. From this high point Hengistbury Head gently slopes down to a height of approximately 15 metres at its eastern end. This gently sloping small plateau is known as Warren Hill. Approximately half way along Warren Hill, the northern aspect of the Head is bisected by a 19th century open cast Iron Ore mine.

During the last ice age (circa 12,000 years ago) Hengistbury Head was several Kilometres inland. At that time the River Stour flowed to the south of Hengistbury Head while the River Avon flowed out to the north. Both of these rivers probably joined into the Grand Solent River that is believed to have meandered through a river valley in an area now occupied by the sea and known as The Solent. This river originally flowed into the sea east of Southampton and was contained by a southerly chalk ridge stretching from the Needles to the Purbecks. Over time the river eroded into the chalk ridge as at the same time the sea cut into the ridge from the south. Eventually the ridge was breached and the Solent River flowed out to the sea somewhere between a line drawn between the Needles and Old Harry Rock. Further erosion took place and over time the whole ridge was destroyed. This left the softer soils behind the ridge directly at the mercy of the sea. As sea levels rose the whole of this river valley flooded and left us with the expanse of water now known as The Solent.

Evidence for the Stour running to the south of the Head lies in alluvial gravels and soils that can be clearly seen in the exposed strata near the Double Dykes. There still exists a small stretch of the old Stour riverbed just south of the main car park. It appears that after the River Stour and the River Avon eroded the ridge that divided them, they joined together north of Hengistbury Head so the final reaches of the River Stour ended up following the same course as the Avon. Another small river began to flow in the old Stour bed, and joined into the Stour/Avon confluence north of Hengistbury Head. This new river flowed in the opposite direction to that originally taken by the River Stour. This would indicate that the Stour and Avon joined up in Christchurch while the Head was still several Kilometres inland and the plain between it and the chalk ridge was capable of providing enough water for this short lived impostor. It is probable that this river was actually the small river that flows through the centre of Bournemouth called the River Bourne. Although today this river flows out to sea several kilometres west of Hengistbury Head, in the past, before coastal erosion, the River Bourne hooked round and must have originally joined the river Stour just south of Hengistbury Head. After the river Stour abandoned its original river course some blockage between the old course and the river Solent must have caused the river Bourne to re-route back up the old River Stour bed and join the Stour and Avon in their joint course north of Hengistbury Head.

The base of the Head is formed from Boscombe Sands, a compressed and soft rocklike sand that is easily friable (crumbles). Above the Boscombe Sands is about 3 metres of greenish sandy clay known as the Lower Hengistbury Head Beds. This is topped with about 15 metres of brown sandy clay. Embedded within this layer are large (up to 2 metres in diameter) boulders of Ironstone. This is known as the Upper Hengistbury Beds. On top of this is about 2 to

3 metres of white compressed sand containing islands of clay. This layer is known as the Highcliffe Beds. A layer of riverbed gravel sits on top of this and is about 1 metre thick. Finally the top of the headland is covered by a thin topsoil that in the main consists of windblown sand. All of the strata are inclined at about 3 degrees to the horisontal (declining to the south-east).

Formations similar to those at Hengistbury Head can be found further along the coast at Highcliffe and also inland at St Catherine's Point which is a similar high ground to Hengistbury Head although it is approximately 3 kilometres inland. St Catherine's Mount, today, probably resembles Hengistbury Head as it was 12,000 years ago.

The Strata of Hengistbury Head

Boscombe Sands

The base of Hengistbury Head is built on a base of compressed yellow sand interspersed with layers of shingle. The overall colour of this soft rock varies from a light grey through to a mauve-brown colour. This colour variation is governed by the amount of organic material present in the rock and also on the moisture content. The sand grains making up the Boscombe Sands are generally rounded or subangular grains of quartz. This type of formation is typical of material deposited on a sea beach. The shingle beds in the lower parts of this layer consist of well rolled flints that show signs of being battered by wave action. These flints are usually white or grey. The sandstone is devoid of large animal fossils because, being laid down on a shallow tidal beach or sandbank, there was no possibility of the animal remains being entombed in the sand and forming fossils. Some of the pitted flints contain small amounts of chalky deposits. The upper layers of the bed contains layers of bleached pebbles which were probably washed down from the surrounding hills to a shallow estuary.

The lower levels of the Boscombe Sands contain minute fossils of the burrows of small crustaceans. Fossils of leaves and other vegetable material have been found but due to the friable nature of the Boscombe Sands they are difficult if not impossible to extract.

The upper levels of the Boscombe Sands indicate that the previous sea beach environment was suffering under continuous flooding and submergence and the tidal and wave action effects which give the lower parts of this strata its disordered structure were becoming less dominant. Instead, without the massive influence of wave and tide the last few centimetres of this stratum take on a more ordered structure with finer grained sediment.

The Boscombe Sands were created during the Eocene time period, which was about 100 million years after the creation of the chalk ridge from Old Harry Rock to the Needles (Mesozoic timescale). This chalk ridge was formed from the collective debris from the shells of tiny crustaceans that built up over millions of years on a sea bed. The area was subject to massive geological forces that forced this chalk stratum upwards. This, coupled with the drop in sea level leaves us with the chalk cliffs we find today.

Boscombe Sands are the oldest part of Hengistbury Head and date back about 50 million years. Dinosaurs never walked on Hengistbury Head as they died out at the end of the Mesozoic period, many millions of years before the Boscombe Sands were laid down. It is interesting to speculate that, as this stratum was laid down on a pre-historic beach, that the layers of flints were probably driven onto the beach by wave action, possibly during storms or other catastrophic events. While the composition and age of these materials is unimaginably vast we can still see unique short-term events in their structure like the flint layers.

An interesting anomaly currently exists on the beach just west of the Double Dykes, A large clay slab lies under the river gravels and in the Boscombe Sands. From the formation of the Boscombe Sands on a sea beach, such a clay slab is out of place. These clay slabs are usually evidence of ponds and lagoons. The clay slab formed the base of the pond. Today this clay base is on the edge of the beach and is covered by the much newer alluvial gravels from the old

Stour/Bourne river bed. It can be seen that this clay base has fared much better under the erosion effects of the sea than has the surrounding gravel and nearby Eocene sandstone deposits. It is probable that this clay slab dates from much later and while predating the river gravels would still be a relatively new structure. It could have been a pond or lake feeding the grand Solent river before it was overwhelmed by the river Stour. Alternatively this clay slab may have been laid down with the Hengistbury Beds and has simply slipped down through the strata as the river eroded the surrounding soft rock.

The Boscombe Sands can be seen as the lowest strata of Hengistbury Head and due to the dip of 3 degrees eastward the stratum disappears below the level of the beach about half way along Hengistbury Head.

Lower Hengistbury Beds

The top of the Boscombe Sands is separated from the Lower Hengistbury Beds by a layer of black flints. This flint layer would indicate a sea invasion that signalled a general sea level rise for at least part of the time period during which the Lower Hengistbury Beds were laid down. The deposits of this new stratum are a maximum of 4 metres in thickness and are mainly Glauconitic sandy clay. Glauconite is a mineral with a greenish/olive colouring.

The type of formation, indicates that it was formed as part of river estuary or delta with surrounding bogs, marshes and swamps. The presence of Glauconite would also back this up. Glauconite is formed from an interaction of fine clumped clay particles with salt water. A river estuary would provide the ideal environment for this reaction to take place between seawater and the debris brought down to the estuary by the river.

This stratum is littered with the fossilised remains of pre-historic tropical and sub-tropical plants and ferns and occasional Lignitic layers can be found as well. Lignite is a woody textured mineral derived from vegetation and is a bit a like a half way house between Peat and Coal. It can be burnt and is often used as fuel, although the deposits at Hengistbury Head are not extensive enough to have provided a significant fuel source.

The Hengistbury Beds used to extend to Alum Bay in the Isle of Wight, which has identical structures to that found on Hengistbury Head. Elsewhere the Hengistbury Beds can be found in the bottom strata of the cliffs off Highcliffe and also in nearby St Catherine's Point.

Upper Hengistbury Beds

The Upper Hengistbury Beds are the most prominent of the stratum. They are approximately 15 metres thick and are a creamy brown colour. The most striking feature of this layer is the existence within it of large Ironstone concretions, known as Ironstone Doggers. These vary in size but usually are at least 1 metre across with some being 2 metres. The Ironstones lie in almost parallel lines, there being between 3 and 5 layers along the cliff edge. These Doggers had provided the main defence against erosion for the last several thousand years. The normal slow erosion that had taken place had caused the Ironstones to form a natural reef-like structure off shore. The boulders had also lined the beach protecting the base of the headland. Because of these natural defences erosion was gradual and possibly stationary. Their removal in the 1690's and the 1850's has been the main cause of the terrible erosion problems now found at Hengistbury Head.

These Ironstone boulders were formed in a stagnant bog environment. Iron compounds were washed down by the river and formed a layer on the bed of an estuary. As the sea level rose and fell the layer of Iron compounds congregated into clumps and a chemical reaction with a reducing agent (probably Carbon from decayed vegetation) left the Iron Ore nodules we have today. The layering took place on many occasions and some of the Doggers have layers like an onion. Within these layers have been found fossilised sharks teeth, vertebrae and unidentified vegetable matter. These concretions or Doggers were probably shifted from their point of creation to their locations with the Upper Hengistbury Beds by flooding and storm. Below the bottom layer of Doggers the Hengistbury Beds show signs of fossilised worm and crustacean burrows similar to those found in the Boscombe Sands.

The Upper Hengistbury Head beds also appear east of Hengistbury Head in the lower stratum of the cliffs at Highcliffe. However there appear to be no Doggers in this area. A similar structure can be found at St Catherine's Point, about 3 kilometres inland from Hengistbury Head. Here the stratum is only a metre or two from the top of the structure. This layer does have some Ironstones embedded in it.

Highcliffe Beds

The Highcliffe Beds mark the top layer of the Eocene strata on Hengistbury Head. Like the Boscombe Sands this layer appears to have been laid down on a sea beach and has a similar structure to that of the Boscombe Sands. Small areas of clay can be found in this layer. These are from the river erosion of clay patches that were previously the base of small lagoons or ponds. The clumps of clay were washed and rolled down by a river and ended up being washed up onto the beach by wave action. The clay lumps then became incorporated into the general make up of the beach. This layer also shows the typical sea beach feature of having bands of pebbles, each band probably indicating a large storm or short sudden incident. The Highcliffe Beds get their name for their more prominent location in the cliffs at Highcliffe, where they form the mid band between the Hengistbury Beds and the Barton sands.

The Upper layers (gravel and top soil)

Due to the proximity of the nearby river systems a great deal of river deposits exist on and around Hengistbury Head. These river deposits consist mainly of river gravels and are some of the newest of the deposits at the Head.

During the last million years a succession of ice ages have been interspersed by warmer sub Mediterranean style weather. During the cold periods large quantities of water became locked up in ice and consequently the sea level dropped. At other times the ice melted and the sea level rose. At the beginning of this period this rise could be as much as 200 metres. Due to the lowering sea level during the ice ages, rivers flowing into the sea had to cut down into their beds to reach the new lower level, this left their former river gravels suspended above the new river bed in a terrace. The new river course flooded during the warmer periods when the ice melted and raised the sea level. The process repeated when the next ice age started. Depending on the duration and the severity of the cold periods the grading (cutting down) of the valley floor varied. The net result is a series of river terraces in a river valley. Three such terraces exist on Hengistbury Head and there is also the newer river gravels from the former river Stour channel and the existing river system.

The first and newest of these structure exists west of the Double Dykes and is the former bed of the river Stour. After the river Avon and river Stour eroded their dividing ridge and joined in a confluence about 1 kilometre north-west of the Head the old river Stour bed, which used to route the river to the south of Hengistbury Head, was adopted by the river Bourne. Today the river Bourne flows through the middle of Bournemouth and enters the sea is a South-easterly direction. During the last ice age, when the area now occupied by Poole Bay was a river valley, the river Bourne used to continue further south and then hook round and flow into the confluence of the rivers Avon and Stour from a north-easterly direction.

The abandoned river bed West of the Double Dykes is therefore the product of two rivers, each flowing in the opposite direction to the other. This river bed shows the typical formations expected from a river bed. The bed consists of sharp angled flints mixed in with coarse sand. The texture is similar to that of builder's concrete aggregate before mixing in the cement. The whole mass is a sandy orange in colour. These river deposits, mainly from the river Stour and river Bourne date back about 10,000 years and are among the newest deposits at Hengistbury Head.

The River Terraces

The three river terraces that sit on Hengistbury Head have been named after similar structures found near London although there is no direct correlation between them. These three terraces are:

The Boyne River Terrace

The oldest river deposits on Hengistbury Head are on the top of Warren Hill. These gravels are known as the Boyne Hill River Terrace. This layer of gravels is probably of the order of 200,000 years old. It should be realised that this means that 200,000 years ago, far from being a piece of high ground this area of Hengistbury Head was actually the bottom of a river valley (the river bed in fact!). It would have been surrounded by higher ground. The whole area would have been unrecognisable to that of today.

The Lower Taplow River Terrace

The set of gravels known as the Lower Taplow terrace converges with the Boyne Terrace at Warren Hill but mainly occupies the eastern side of Warren hill. This would have been formed as the sea levels dropped and forced the river to cut down into its bed leaving the previous bed high and dry. However the surrounding area would have still been generally higher than Hengistbury Head.

The second Lower Taplow terrace

The newest set of gravels that actually sit on the Head are the Second Lower Taplow terrace. These sit about half way down the Head on the northern escarpment. These gravels have been disturbed and covered by the spoil from the old open cast mine from the Hengistbury Mining Company. This area is now known as the Batters. Again this terrace would have been formed due to a further drop in sea level, causing the river to grade down further from its original bed.

Topsoil

The other remaining deposit on Hengistbury Head is the topsoil. The majority of the topsoil on both the Head itself and on the land surrounding it is made up from windblown sand and has a depth of about one metre. Areas in front of and behind the most eastern of the Double Dykes have a depth of up to three metres.

New Deposits

While Hengistbury Head has suffered massive erosion in recent times, there has also been deposition of materials on both the south-easterly beach and the northern shore line. The deposits on the northern shore line of Hengistbury Head are traditional river deposits leading to the building of salt marshes and reed beds. These are most prominent to the west of the Double Dykes where they form the Wickhams. Further east, in front of the quarry there has also been a similar building of new land. These areas are called the Salt Hurns and Rushy Piece. An interesting (though unrelated) item in this area is a deeper area of the harbour just off the Salt Hurns called Lob's Hole. Lob's Hole is caused by a fresh water spring that breaks out into the harbour bottom and is only visible as a spring at very low tides.

The building of materials off the south-easterly aspect of the Head has been deliberately caused by the building of a set of groynes. The purpose of these groynes is to reverse the damage done by the removal of the Ironstones in the mid 19th century. The main build up of material has been to the west of the major breakwater built at the easterly extremity of Hengistbury Head in 1938. Here there has been a major deposit of sand and shingle from long shore drift and the beach now probably extends out to close to its position in the late 19th century. The beach close in to the Head has turned into a sand dune structure with grasses growing and further stabilising the immediate area.

History of Hengistbury Head.

Upper Palaeolithic Period (pre 7500BC)

The occupation of Hengistbury Head dates back to about 10,000 BC. Some significant finds from this period have been made at Hengistbury Head. This first period of occupation falls into a period known as the Old Stone Age or Upper Palaeolithic period. . During most of this time the English Channel had yet to be completely flooded and Hengistbury Head lay on the edge of a large river valley (the river Solent) with the sea many Kilometres distant beyond the Chalk ridge stretching from the Needles to the Old Harry Rocks. Until the discovery and containment of fire, the succession of ice ages made this area generally too cold for human habitation and visitors were nomadic and occasional. The cold weather inhibited the growth of forests and the terrain must have been bleak and inhospitable. Around the Dorset locality, many finds from the Upper Palaeolithic period have been made, but only a few match those of the quality found at Hengistbury Head.

These finds at Hengistbury Head probably relate to a group or groups of nomadic hunters that camped on the high ground offered by the Head. The Head was near the river Solent and some of its main tributaries (including the river Avon and river Stour) and must have been close to watering and migration routes for Deer, Bison, Horses and possibly Mammoths. These people probably followed the migration paths of their prey and had several semi fixed camps that they used through the seasons. These people had only stone tools and weapons but they were very skilful in their manufacture. Some prize examples have been found at Hengistbury Head, mainly on the top of Warren hill. These flint, bone and antler tools formed

The approach to Hengistbury Head from the West

The Westward view from Warren Hill

The crumbling cliff face of Hengistbury Head clearly shows the strata that form the Head. A new fall of talus on the left shows erosion continues. Iron stone Doggers would have slowed this erosion

A permanent scar on Hengistbury Head is the northern end of the 19th century Iron stone quarry

The southern end of the quarry has been
turned into a scenic lake. The lake is too
acidic for many forms of vegetation but a
great deal of wildlife is supported. In the
Summer the lake often turns bright green
due to algal bloom.

Some of the Iron Stone
Doggers have layers like an
onion.

Ironstone doggers have fallen to the beach as the cliff has receded. Where there are doggers on the beach the erosion is slowed. . Also note two parallel rows of doggers in the Upper Hengistbury Beds about half way up the cliff face

The stunted forest to the north of the Head is one of the oldest forests in the country

the every day tools these people needed such as scrapers, spear Heads and knives. Hengistbury Head is one of only 25 sites from this period found in this country. The majority of the finds have been in or near caves. Only 4 non cave sites have so far been identified, including the one at Hengistbury Head. Unfortunately the main archaeological site was right on the cliff edge and has been lost due to erosion. However most of the artifacts were recovered prior to this loss.

Mesolithic Period(7500 -4000 BC)

As the last ice age of the Upper Palaeolithic period came to an end the climate became warm and moist. This change in climate led a major change in to the type of vegetation that dominated this area and large tracks of previously open grassland turned into dense forest. Most people of that period lived along the coast or along rivers, as the development of these thick forests over England made inland penetration difficult. It should be remembered that Hengistbury Head was at this time still a fair way inland from the sea and consequently was probably only rarely visited by passing hunters. The advantages of the high ground offered by Hengistbury Head to the nomadic people of this time were exactly the same as those offered to their forebears from the Old Stone Age. The people from this age were, however more skilled in the manufacture of weapons and tools. Hundreds of skilfully honed flints have been found from this period, again on the cliff edge on Warren Hill. These finds are midway along Warren hill whereas the Old Stone Age finds were towards the eastern end of the Head.

Neolithic Period (4000 - 2000 BC)

The heavy forestation period of the Mesolithic period led people to congregate along the coastlines and move away from the typical nomadic hunter-gatherer lifestyle. This proceeded through to the Neolithic period (or New Stone Age) which had communities now following a more static lifestyle, as herdsmen and farmers. Gradually they moved inland forming settlements as they went. Great numbers of early Neolithic stone implements have been found on the Head although there is currently no direct evidence for occupation. It is believed that there was a substantial settlement from this period on Hengistbury Head. The range and variety of the finds made to date make Hengistbury Head one of the most important archaeological sites in the UK from this period. Towards the end of this period other imported good began to appear in the Christchurch area. Several tools made from non local stones have been found that indicates that trade had developed between the people living in the Christchurch area and with communities in Devon and France.

Bronze Age (2000 BC - 600 BC)

Several Tumuli (burial mounds) that date from the early part of this period have been discovered on the lowlands of Hengistbury Head. These tumuli have been found to contain the cremated remains of people, thought to be important local individuals. Other items found in the tumuli include various pottery and animal remains. It is believed that part of Hengistbury Head was essentially an early Bronze Age cemetery, at least for the local rich. A great deal of archaeologically valuable material has been retrieved from the funeral barrows and the materials discovered are typical of what is known as Wessex culture or early Bronze Age. An interesting feature of the barrows on Hengistbury Head that was disclosed by the two main archaeological investigations of Bushe-Fox (1913-15) and Gray (1922) is that the barrows all contained a scattering of earlier flint tools and weapons. This would indicate that the barrows were built upon land that had been previously occupied, so the cemetery only appeared after the Head and vicinity had been settled. Towards the end of this period it appears (from the lack of finds) that the Head was either sparsely populated or abandoned completely for a period of several hundred years.

Iron Age (600BC - 400AD)

The most spectacular feature from this period on Hengistbury Head is the massive earthworks on the neck of the isthmus leading up to the Head. The design of the earthworks (known as the Double Dykes) is very reminiscent of similar protective schemes found at Badbury Rings and Maiden Castle and date from approximately 100 BC. The defensive advantage of Hengistbury Head was that the earthworks were only needed on one side as the Head itself provided defensive high ground. It is likely that at this time the sea had advanced to within 500 metres of its current position. An early hand drawn map of Hengistbury Head made in the 1700's indicates that at that time the earthworks curved around the Head and down to the sea. It is interesting to speculate how far these earthworks actually extended when they were first made over 2000 years ago, one imagines that their true length and form must have been much more significant than that remaining today.

The close proximity of high grade Iron ore in the Ironstone Doggers on the southern beach, coupled with a ready supply of charcoal raised Hengistbury Head's status. It rapidly became a primary trading port importing wine, tools and pottery from as far away as Italy. A great deal of metal working was conducted at the Head, not just of Iron but of silver and bronze. Many coins have been found, interestingly some of which appear to be forgeries with a bronze base given a dip coating of silver!

The Roman Period 43AD - 500 AD

The advent of Roman rule in 43 AD had little effect on the trading activities of Hengistbury Head, indeed locally minted coins appear to have remained in circulation for over a hundred years after the Romans had landed. Perhaps because of its remoteness from Roman authority and maybe because it posed no threat to Roman rule it appears that Hengistbury Head was generally left in peace. However greater effect was felt indirectly as Rome closed its grip on the trading partners of Hengistbury Head. The Roman occupation of Gaul led to a marked decrease of trading from Gaul (France) to English settlements like Hengistbury Head and subsequently had an effect upon Hengistbury trading patterns.

Trade from the Head declined over the Roman period, probably as trade relocated to centres nearer Roman influence and wealth. Less than 100 Roman coins have been found on Hengistbury Head.

The ending of the Roman occupation around 450 AD parallelled the final decay and abandonment of habitation of Hengistbury Head. Why this final abandonment occurred is uncertain. Iron ore was in abundant supply and the harbour was still functional. While international trade conducted from Hengistbury Head had been in decline since the arrival of the Romans, there was still a viable industrial centre. The abandonment was possibly due to intimidation from Saxon and Jutish raiders or more probably due to the relocation of both trade and manufacture to larger centres of population.

The end of Roman occupation of England saw Hengistbury Head return to wilderness and seclusion for several hundred years.

The Middle Ages and Hengistbury Head

Hengistbury Head probably passed the first few centuries of the first millennium as little more than a lonely headland, several hundred metres from the sea, visited solely by occasional hunters. Due to the marginality of the soil and its remoteness few people spent time there. The population of the whole of England at this time was only a few million and poor quality farming land like Hengistbury Head must have figured far down their list of preferred sites.

The next utilisation of the site did not occur until the 9th century when Alfred the Great sought to re-vitalise the harbour in defence of Wessex against the continental raiders of that time. Alfred constructed a Burgh (defensive settlement) on the site now occupied by the town of Christchurch and no doubt Hengistbury Head became a lookout for the defence of Wessex, although no data from this period has yet been found at the Head.

Hengistbury Head is first described as Hedensburia in the late 11th century in a document granting Christchurch Priory domain over Hedensburia and all that is adjacent. The grantor was Baldwin de Redvers, the Lord of the Manor of Christchurch, Twyneam.

Hengistbury Head in the 16th Century

Hengistbury Head was known as Hynebury or simply Christchurch Head(s) in the 16th century. It only became known as Hengistbury Head after the discovery of stone and Iron Age artifacts. Being inspired by romanticism rather than actual evidence, and distracted by the 11th century reference to Hedenesburia gave the gentry of the time inspiration to re-name Hynebury after Hengist, hence Hengistbury Head. Interestingly Smeaton, in his report on possible harbour improvements (see later) refers to Hengistbury Head or Heads and then goes on to describe a dual prominence with a small inlay or bay between them. It would appear that today one of the these Headlands has been totally lost and that Hengistbury Head was really Hengistbury Heads (or Christchurch Heads) prior to the 17th century.

Hengistbury Head in the 17th Century

Christchurch has always been a shallow drying harbour with difficult access. During the mid 1600's, Andrew Yarranton outlined a scheme to improve Christchurch Harbour. Yarranton planned to utilise the ready supply of Iron Ore from the Doggers at Hengistbury Head to build a naval gunnery foundry and, utilising existing boat and ship building facilities, to build a naval dockyard. A fort was planned to aid local defence and he also planned to make the river Avon more navigable so goods could be transported further inland with ease. Under the sponsorship of the Lord of the Manor of Christchurch, (Lord Clarendon, the Chancellor of Charles II) Yarranton produced a document detailing his proposals. Most of Yarranton's proposals came to nothing. The one major item of the Yarranton scheme that came to being was to cut a deep water channel from the harbour out to the sea, avoiding the treacherous narrow entrance to Christchurch Harbour (locally known as the Run). The channel was cut through Mudeford spit approximately half way along this being about 600 metres from the Head . It was in use by 1698. Yarranton utilised the boulders from the Head to build a jetty out from the cut. While the cut provided direct access to deeper water avoiding the fast flowing Run and the treacherous sandbanks at its entrance, the cut suffered from long shore drift where sand collected against the jetty and narrowed down the cut. Evidently Yarranton cut was in use for up to 30 years but was blocked on several occasions, the most severe problems occurring after the great storm of 1703. It was finally abandoned after it was blocked by yet another heavy storm. Yarranton made the rather obvious and severe mistake of building his pier on the northern side of the cut, this caused the pier to capture the long shore drift sand and block the channel, which was only kept clear by the strength of the river flow and dredging. If he had build his pier to the south of the cut things may have been different. Only the line of Ironstone Doggers now remain which mark Yarranton brave attempt.

Locally the line of the old jetty is known as Clarendons Jetty or the Long Rocks. Whether Yarranton cut actually caused the closure of the original exit is doubtful, in any event things rapidly returned to the original natural state with the two rivers flowing out through the Run and Yarranton's cut filled in by the wind and sea. Today there is no indication of the cut save the Long Rocks. Clarendons Jetty must have used many hundreds if not thousands of tons of the Ironstone Doggers from Hengistbury Head. One would expect that they were collected in the easiest manner available and were probably stripped off one small area of the foreshore, exposing the friable base of one of the Heads to the action of the sea at that point. Smeaton, in a report 90 years later, indicates that severe erosion was being experienced by Hengistbury Head. Currently the manmade damage to the Head is solely attributed to John Holloway and the Hengistbury Mining Co (see later) but possibly the first blow was delivered over 150 years earlier by the building of Clarendon's Jetty.

Through probably not related to Yarranton's scheme but dating from the same period, is the Black House at the north end of the Island (Mudeford spit), a place known as Gervis Point. The Black house was a centre for shipbuilding with several ships over 100 tons being built. The western (harbour facing) wall of this building was used as a support for partially built vessels. They were launched directly into the deep water of the Run.

The Black house mirrored its contemporary across the Run, the Haven House tavern. Incidentally the current Haven House tavern is actually is an impostor dating back a mere 150 years or so. The original Haven House Inn on Mudeford Quay was the building now known as the Dutch House. The Dutch House was used to accommodate some of the Dutch engineers brought in to construct Clarendon Jetty and the associated cut through Mudeford Spit. Some of these Dutchmen engraved their names into some of the windows of the Dutch house and evidently these engravings can still be seen today.

Hengistbury Head in the 18th Century

After the demise of Yarranton's scheme the harbour reverted to being a small fishing port and the Head (or Heads) no doubt, reverted to a desolate piece of marginal grazing land. However in 1733 The Walpole government passed the Excise and Customs Bill. This severely restricted the import of a whole range of items into the country, and imposed punitive levies on items such as Brandy, wine, silk and lace. The local fishing and farming fraternity (and just about everyone else for that matter!) took to smuggling or aiding and abetting the smugglers. The smugglers became known rather more pleasantly as Free Traders. Hengistbury Head due to its anonymous and remote location played a central part in this smuggling. Bizarrely the ancient defensive rampart, the Double Dykes, were put to use by the smugglers as they provided almost perfect cover for trains of wagons used to take away the casks of Brandy and wine. A great deal of contraband was landed either off the seaward side of Hengistbury Head or brought up through the Run and landed off at the Wickhams or through Mother Sillers Channel in Stanpit Marsh. The contraband landed off the Wickhams or off the seaward side of the Head was generally then taken by cart up through what is now Bournemouth ands offloaded of various farms, taverns and private houses as the entourage went by. The contraband offloaded at Mother Sillers channel usually made its way to the Ship In Distress at Mudeford. Mother Sillers channel is named after one the Landladies of The Ship in Distress, namely Hanna Siller, a notorious smuggler and dealer in contraband who had started her career at the original Haven House tavern on Mudeford Quay.

Smuggling was to continue off Hengistbury Head until the mid 1850's. The most dramatic event of these times occurred in 1784 when the so called Battle of Mudeford took place. This involved the planned interception of a smuggler off Hengistbury Head (or Christchurch Point as the contemporary description described it). The smugglers where evidently under the command of "Slippery Rogers", the grandson of the former mayor of Christchurch.

Long boats were being unloaded on the beach as the coastguard cutter arrived on the scene, a battle ensued that cost the lives of many of the coastguard as well as the smugglers. As a result some smugglers were press-ganged into the poorly staffed Royal Navy others were transported and at least one was hanged.

During this period, as the smuggling continued apace, a scheme emulating or exceeding Yarrantons original 17th century ideas were put forward. In 1762, John Smeaton placed proposals forward to enhance Christchurch harbour and aid navigation from Christchurch to Salisbury via the river Avon. He favoured a cut through the Mudeford spit, as had Yarranton. Smeaton though, understood the nature of long shore drift and laid plans to build the southern jetty before the northern one and also to ensure that length of the southern jetty was much greater than that of the northern one. Smeaton planned to use the Ironstone Doggers from the Head and to supplement these with cheap low quality stone from Portland. Had Smeatons scheme gone ahead then it is likely that the catastrophic damage done by Iron ore extraction in the 1850's would have been pre-empted by Smeaton. The extra one hundred years of heavy erosion would have probably spelt extinction for the Head. If this development had actually taken place the whole of the coastline between the Old Harry Rocks and Hirst Castle would now be dramatically different. Smeaton estimated the cost the engineering works at about £6000. Whether the financial cost was deemed too high is unknown but, for whatever reason, Smeatons plans were abandoned.

Hengistbury Head in the 19th Century

The smuggling continued and arguably was at its height in the early 1800's. It was not until the 1850's that the government gained the upper hand and smuggling became a rarity rather than the norm.

As smuggling ended other uses for the Head came to the fore. A local coal merchant by the name of George Holloway found a way of mitigating the loss of profit on returning empty coal barges. He gained mining rights from the Lord of the Manor who claimed foreshore rights (although these are normally attributed to the Crown) and exploited the Ironstone Doggers found at the Head. These were initially used as ballast on the barges back to Southampton. They were then transferred to the larger coal ships trading from Cardiff (again as ballast) and finally delivered to the blast furnaces of Merthyr Tydfil and the Rhondda in South Wales. Essentially Mr. Holloway was simply adding a layer of efficiency to his main activity as a coal merchant. Unfortunately his dredging of the waters off the Head coupled with the removal of the easily won Ironstone Doggers off the southern beach led to a massive de-stabilisation of geological forces that maintained the Head at a steady but slow erosion rate. Suddenly the sea was able to batter the base of the cliff and carry away the sand . In addition to the removal of the sea and beach Iron ore deposits, an open cast mine was set up approximately half way along the Head. The gains from all three were shipped out via Holloways Dock, a small quay set up in what is now marsh land at the joint of the Head with the Mudeford spit. The spoil from the open cast mining activity was dumped along the north-west side of the Head in an area now known as the Batters.

After the removal of the Ironstone Doggers from the sea and from the beach, rapid erosion of the Head took place. Several reports were issued to the admiralty from sea farers who found the previously sheltered anchorages in Christchurch bay were becoming exposed to the prevailing south-westerly winds. Possibly due to these detrimental effects upon the environment Holloways dredging off Hengistbury Head was halted. The extraction of Iron from the sea had ended by 1856 although further extraction from other places continued until the 1870's. The erosion of Hengistbury Head continued unabated and apparently unnoticed (or at least uncared for) for the next fifty years.

While Holloway was busily mining the Hengistbury Iron ore others were developing schemes for Christchurch harbour.

Reports were made by William Armstrong and John Silvester, but Christchurch Council, after having commissioned these reports, had neither the resources or the willingness to carry them through. The final set of development plans for Christchurch harbour was set forward in 1885 by the Christchurch and Wimborne Railway Company, no doubt intending to develop the rudimentary facilities set up by Holloways Hengistbury mining company. This scheme was by far the grandest, planning a 1000 yard (approx. 800 metre) breakwater to protect the harbour entrance. A major dock would have been set up by Long Field, to the north-east of the Head. A railway line from Wimborne was planned to link up to this dock. However in the end the backers of this scheme withdrew their support and the scheme folded. Interestingly a small vestige of the first stage of this dock may still exist. Just about 50 metres east of the Sail Training Centre, and only accessible via a narrow path through the reed beds, is a small landing stage, currently used as a fishing platform. Whether the original structure is associated with the 1885 scheme or possibly with later work done by the army in World War One I have been unable to discover. The skeletal remains of the old landing seems too substantial to have been set up originally as a mere fishing platform. The flow of the joint rivers Avon and Stour at this point give two channels. The major channel flows close to the north side of the river bank, however the second channel flows down south side of the river bank, hugging the reed beds close to the Sail Training Centre and passing this small stunted dock. The 1885 scheme would have been well placed to utilise the natural depth created by the river, although it is certain that dredging would still have had to have been done to maintain the dock.

Hengistbury Head in the 20th Century

At the beginning of the 20th century (1909) the first significant archaeological finds were made on the north-eastern lowlands of the Head. These finds, coupled with the potential sale of Hengistbury Head to developers by the then owner Sir George Meyrick led a local antiquarian Herbert Druitt to try and save the Head for posterity. He tried to raise interest from the National Trust but to no avail. He then approached the Society of Antiquities in the hope of performing a last excavation to try and save the archaeological history of the Head from developers. Luckily the Society of Antiquities took heed of Herbert Druitts warnings and mounted an excavation under the direction of J.P. Bushe-Fox starting in 1911. Shortly into this excavation it was realised that the nature of the finds being made were very significant and this weighed heavily against proposed developments. A scheme for 80 residential properties to be built just west of the Double Dykes was dropped as was a scheme to construct a golf course on Warren Hill. However some preparation work was done for both of these schemes, mainly involving some ploughing in both areas.

During World War One Hengistbury Head was sold to Mr. Gordon Selfridge. Due to the constraints imposed by the war, development planned by Mr. Selfridge was delayed. Selfridge planned to build a huge mansion on Warren Hill, outline plans of which can be found in the Red House Museum. As part of this scheme a nursery garden was planted in the lee of the Head west of the open cast mine. This exists today, although it has deliberately been left to go wild and now forms a bird sanctuary. Mr. Bushe-Fox published his report in 1915 although other excavations took place through to 1924. Finally Selfridge abandoned the scheme for his residence on the Head and in 1930 sold Hengistbury Head to Bournemouth Borough Council. From then on the Head has been designated a public open space and recreational area. During the period since the closure of the open cast mine in the latter part of the 19th century there had been a catastrophic loss of Headland due to erosion with almost half of the Head having been washed away. All of the spoil from the Head ended up being dumped by long shore drift at the far end of Mudeford spit. It was prevented from piling up against the quay by the river exit known as the Run. Consequently a long spit built up off the Head stretching at times for over a mile from the Black House down to opposite Steamer Lodge. A Cyclic event set up where a storm would trigger the formation of a lagoon which would then slowly fill with sand. This happened a number of times over the years. In 1935 Bournemouth Council took positive action to save Hengistbury Head and built a breakwater out from the eastern tip towards the Beerpan rocks, (these rocks probably mark the original extent of Hengistbury Head before the mining activity caused the rapid erosion). At the same time and arguably more environmentally detrimental, Bournemouth Borough Council built an access road to Hengistbury Head. This brought many visitors to the Head along with a new set of environmental pressures. Since then, to aid the visitors and also reduce the damage from trampling, a number of paths have been laid. A visitors centre along with a café has been built and the low level path from the Head to the north end of Mudeford Spit has been surfaced although only approved vehicles are allowed to use this narrow road. A Land or Noddy train runs from the visitor centre to the Island, although the walk is much prettier. Two large car parks exist along with some parking along the access road (The Broadway). Generally, today, in summer the area is saturated with vehicles. Many people utilise the beaches on the seaward side although there is a low level of usage of the harbour side of the Head except at the north end of the Island where there are a set of moorings. Mudeford Spit itself, once a mass of huge dunes has been colonised by a great number of huts and now resembles a small shanty town. Because of the beauty of the surrounding area these little huts change hands for many tens of thousands of pounds. A strong community has built up among the hut owners who take great pride in their environment. The major paths on Hengistbury Head have all now been surfaced to prevent further erosion from trampling. Ironically Holloway's Dock, which was the main conduit for the removal of the Ironstone Doggers is now a protected area supporting a range of rare plants and wildlife.

Coastal protection schemes

Erosion problems

Erosion has been a continuous factor at Hengistbury Head since the sea finally reached its base a few thousand years ago. However the natural defence provided by the Ironstones, and possibly other structures (now removed and described later) west of Hengistbury Head ensured that this erosion was slow, if not stationary, for the last two thousand years. Unfortunately a number of catastrophic man made events have taken place, mainly in the last 150 years but starting in the late 17th century. These events have destabilised both Poole and Christchurch bays and although remedial action has alleviated the situation, continued erosion occurs at Hengistbury Head.

Why there is erosion

The major erosion mechanisms effecting Hengistbury Head are driven by the sea and the wind. Before the current sea defences were installed, the sea has direct access to the base of the Head. In storm conditions wave action on the soft rocks of the Head caused sections of the Head to collapse. The prevailing wind in this region is from the south-west. This means that the waves break on the shore at an oblique angle, and becomes mixed with the sand grains. These waves then reflect off the beach moving the sandgrains both out to sea and to the east. It the sand loaded in the incident wave was more than that contained in the reflected wave then the beach would build. If the number of grains in the incident wave was the same as that in the reflect wave then the beach would   maintain itself. However if there are on average more grains in the reflected wave than in the incident wave then the beach will suffer erosion. This is what has happened to Hengistbury Head in the past. Eventually after many cycles of being landed and washed away the grains pass round the eastern end of Hengistbury Head and end up getting dumped on the end of Mudeford sandspit. This mechanism is called Long Shore Drift. As the sand grains are removed they are replaced by the soft rock (talus) from the fallen cliff face. This is soon reduced to fine sand and is consequently washed away in an easterly direction as described above. The exception to this were the Ironstone Doggers. They were generally too heavy to be shifted by the sea and so formed a defensive barrier on the beach reducing the power of the incoming waves. Because of these Doggers the sea failed to reach the base of the cliff and the beach was maintained in a stable state. The removal of the Doggers in 1690 and more significantly in the 1850's were the main reason for the catastrophic erosion that has taken place. However there are other reasons that have possibly contributed to this state of affairs involving development further west.

One factor that has exacerbated the long shore drift erosion at the Head has been the flattening and of the profile of Poole Bay. As Hengistbury Head has receded the incident south-westerly long shore drift has been at an ever shallowing angle. This coupled with such things as the removal of a clay Headland which protruded out to sea and formed a small cove (to facilitate the installation of the cliff lift in the early 1900's) and the concreting of Bournemouth Beach promenade has significantly worsened this problem.

The clay Headland must have provided a natural groyne and essentially broke the bay in to two halves thus reducing the radius of each half of the bay and making each half less prone to long shore drift driven from the prevailing wind. Bournemouth cliffs have also been the victim to massive erosion, their structure is similar to that of Hengistbury Head in being compressed sandy deposits. It recorded that a lady rode a horse up the Bournemouth cliffs in the early 1850's. While this may have been a daring feat it would indicate that the cliffs, at that time were at an angle of no more than 45 degrees. It would seem reasonable that Bournemouth cliffs suffered rapid erosion at roughly the same time as that on Hengistbury Head. The only common factor here is the removal of the Ironstone Doggers. This coupled with the fact that Poole bay had been stable for about 2000 years would indicate the removal of the Doggers has caused an instability in not just at Hengistbury Head but in the whole bay. Bournemouth Cliffs have been stabilised by the construction of a concrete promenade and by the building of a set of long groynes. The consequent containment of loss of material from Bournemouth beaches essentially increased the erosion at Hengistbury Head as the arrival of material from the South-west decreased . The building of groynes at Hengistbury has contained this loss. Currently it has been noticed that there is loss of material from Studland and there has also been considerable loss from cliffs further to the east at Highcliffe and Barton.. Meanwhile the waxing and waning on the sand spit trailing off Hengistbury Head continues, no doubt now supplied by the fine Studland beaches.

While the defences built to protect the Bournemouth beaches and Hengistbury Head have significantly slowed the erosion it is difficult to see how the old pre 1850 'near' equilibrium can now be restored.

The future of Hengistbury Head

In the long run of things Hengistbury Head is doomed to be washed into the sea. Even without the removal of the Ironstone Doggers the eventual long term prognosis was one of erosion and final destruction, although before the damage, this final destruction was far into the future.

Bournemouth council has put a great deal of effort into restoring the equilibrium that was so disastrously disturbed by the mining at Hengistbury Head. This has been generally successful and the council should be congratulated on their tenacious attempts at protecting Hengistbury Head.

The worst case scenario (at least in the short term) would involve a breach of the lowland just east of the Double Dykes so that the sea funnelled down the old Stour/Bourne river bed and through to the Wickhams or through to Barn Bight. This would create Hengistbury Island and would expose a large section of Christchurch harbour and the shoreline at Mudeford to wave action and the prevailing South-westerly wind. One imagines that such an event would also expose Hengistbury Head to erosion from another quarter. Bearing in mind that at the point of this breach the geological makeup of the Head is simply loose river gravel then the erosion would be rapid and catastrophic. A breach would also enable the Avon/Stour river system to exit using the old Stour river bed. Another possibility would then be that Christchurch Harbour, lacking the scouring effect from the river system, would simply silt up and turn to marshland.

To counter this threat the council has erected a wall of galvanised rock filled cages called a Gabion Revetment. This wall is hardly a thing of beauty but it should provide a respite for the lowlands to the west of the Head.

The other main defences erected by the council have been a set of beach groynes that are intended to trap sand and contain the long shore drift that has been the main erosive action in the area. This generally has proved satisfactory, especially at the eastern end of the Head where a large beach, complete with sand dunes has formed.

Another defence mechanism used at Hengistbury Head is beach replenishment using imported shingle. Every decade many tons of shingle are dumped on the beach below Warren Hill and spread over the beach by bull dozers. This is intended to both inhibit Long Shore Drift as well as providing a sacrificial source for the erosion. Unfortunately the concept of beach replenishment has caused a great deal of animosity between Bournemouth Council and those who wish to see a soft sandy beach.

Other ideas have been mooted that could aid the defences of Hengistbury Head. The most popular at the time of writing is for an artificial reef to be built off Southbourne. The purpose of this reef would be to form a shallow area that would in turn build waves for the sport of Surfing. If this reef was moved a little to the east it could possibly form a defensive structure for Hengistbury Head as well as providing a tourist attraction.

There are plans to close the access road along with the sunken car park and to move the whole of the main access point to the Head about 800 metres to the west. This, by reducing direct access will hopefully reduce the man made damage to the Head caused by trampling.

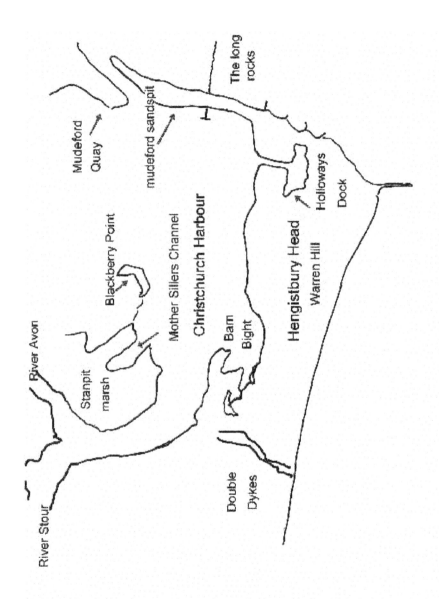

River Avon

River Stour

Stanpit marsh

Blackberry Point

Mother Sillers Channel

Christchurch Harbour

Mudeford Quay

mudeford sandspit

The long rocks

Holloways Dock

Hengistbury Head

Warren Hill

Barn Bight

Double Dykes

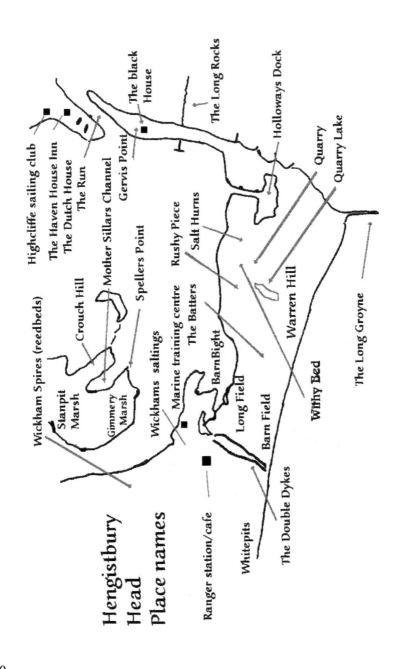

Hengistbury Head Place names

- Highcliffe sailing club
- The Haven House Inn
- The Dutch House
- The Run
- Mother Sillars Channel
- Gervis Point
- The black House
- The Long Rocks
- Holloways Dock
- Quarry
- Quarry Lake
- Spellers Point
- Rushy Piece
- Salt Hurns
- Crouch Hill
- Wickham Spires (reedbeds)
- The Batters
- Warren Hill
- Stanpit Marsh
- Gimmery Marsh
- Wickhams saltings
- Marine training centre
- BarnBight
- The Long Groyne
- Long Field
- Barn Field
- Withy Bed
- Ranger station/cafe
- Whitepits
- The Double Dykes

Hengistbury Head Geology

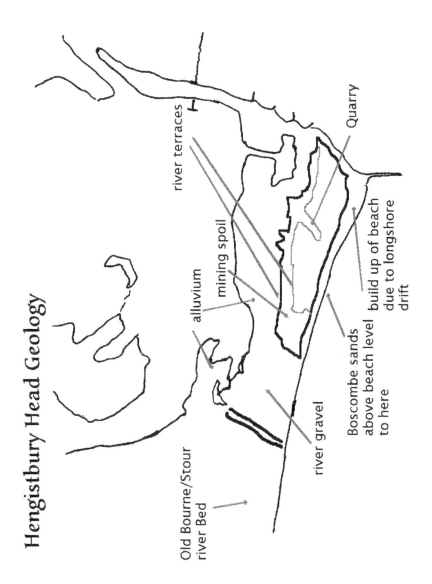

river terraces

Quarry

mining spoil

alluvium

build up of beach
due to longshore
drift

Boscombe sands
above beach level
to here

river gravel

Old Bourne/Stour
river Bed

The Grand Solent River

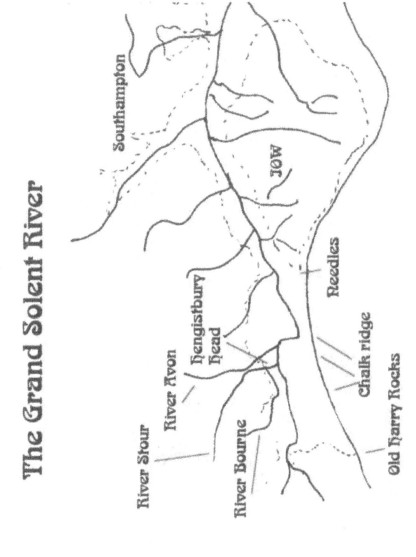

River Stour

River Avon

Hengistbury Head

River Bourne

Southampton

IOW

Needles

Chalk ridge

Old Harry Rocks

Hengistbury Head circa 1700

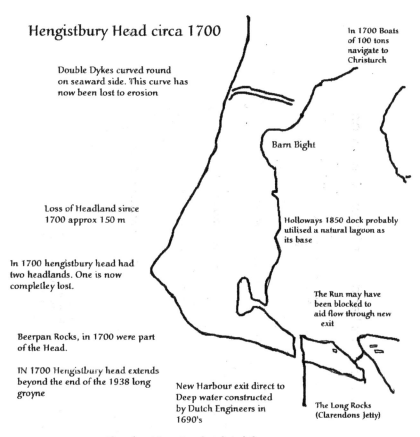

Double Dykes curved round on seaward side. This curve has now been lost to erosion

In 1700 Boats of 100 tons navigate to Christurch

Barn Bight

Loss of Headland since 1700 approx 150 m

Holloways 1850 dock probably utilised a natural lagoon as its base

In 1700 hengistbury head had two headlands. One is now completley lost.

The Run may have been blocked to aid flow through new exit

Beerpan Rocks, in 1700 were part of the Head.

IN 1700 Hengistbury head extends beyond the end of the 1938 long groyne

New Harbour exit direct to Deep water constructed by Dutch Engineers in 1690's

The Long Rocks (Clarendons Jetty)

Clarendons jetty captures longshore drift so new cut silts up. It is in use for no more than 20 years before being abandoned

The long rocks were constructed from Iron Stone Doggers taken off the beach at Hengistbury Head. This was the first step in the de-stabilisation of the Poole/Christchurch Bays that has led to the massive erosion of Hengistbury Head

Hengistbury Island - after a Breach

Stampit Marsh
Recedes

Mudeford suffers
land loss

Christchurch harbour

Breach through Barn Bight

Hengistbury Island

Final course of the two
rivers unknown, they may
route out to sea as
before.or follow a route
out through the breach.This
could have further serious
consequences for the
harbour.

Main point of entry near
the Old Stour river bed

Without the sea defences that have been built up since
1938 this is roughly what would have happened, either by
now, or in the near future. All this damage would have
been directly caused by mans actions in removing the
Iron Stone Doggers off the beach at Hengistbury Head in
the 1850's